THE MANAGING DIFFICULT PARTICIPANTS POCKETBOOK

By John Townsend

Drawings by Phil Hailstone

"All the challengers I have met with are in here - and so are articulate, well-practised and pragmatic replies."
Peter Thomas, Manager, UKBS Career Development and Training

"I loved the book. It shows such a great variety of ways to deal with challengers that everyone will find approaches which will fit their style."
Dr. Martin Gillo, Director, Human Resources, Europe, Advanced Micro Devices

Many thanks to 'Master Trainer' Charles Brulhart for his invaluable help in preparing this Pocketbook. Thanks also to Viviane Jacot for helping us clarify our thoughts.

Published by:
Management Pocketbooks Ltd
Laurel House, Station Approach,
Alresford, Hants SO24 9JH, U.K.
Tel: +44 (0)1962 735573
Fax: +44 (0)1962 733637
E-mail: sales@pocketbook.co.uk
Website: www.pocketbook.co.uk

First edition 1994 (Challengers Pocketbook)
Reprinted as Managing Difficult Participants
2007, ISBN 978 1 903776 22 3

This edition 2010, ISBN 978 1 906610 29 6

© John Townsend 1994, 2007, 2010

British Library Cataloguing-in-Publication
Data – A catalogue record for this book is
available from the British Library.

Design, typesetting and graphics by **efex ltd**.
Printed in U.K.

CONTENTS

DIFFICULT SITUATIONS

DIFFICULT SITUATIONS

CASE STUDY 1

You are a trainer and just about to start a two-day course which has some clear objectives. One of the objectives you have stated on the programme outline is that participants 'will enjoy the learning experience'.

One assertive-looking participant has been reading through the programme outline and, before you can even say, 'Good morning everyone', looks round at the other participants and says loudly: 'It says here that we are supposed to enjoy ourselves on this course. If I'm going to enjoy myself, I shall be the one to decide and not you - is that clear?'

What do you do?

DIFFICULT SITUATIONS

CASE STUDY 2

You are half-way through the first part of a course which, as a professional trainer, you know quite well.

Suddenly one of the participants, a young woman of 30 or so, interrupts you and says: 'Excuse me, I've been sitting here listening to you for the last two hours and every example you have given has concerned a man. I'm really fed up with this sexist attitude. When are you going to realise that men are not alone on this earth!'

What will you do?

DIFFICULT SITUATIONS

CASE STUDY 3

You are running a seminar which you enjoy when suddenly two participants start whispering to each other.

It's the first time it's happened so far and you're not sure whether the whispering is supportive or mischievous.

How would you handle the situation?

DIFFICULT SITUATIONS

CASE STUDY 4

You are the chairperson of a meeting with a project team of cross-functional specialists.

One of the participants is an exceptionally bright male Ph.D. from the Research and Development department. He is getting impatient because of the slow pace of the meeting. He keeps looking at his watch, tapping his pen on the table and giving non-verbal 'hurry up' signals whenever someone expresses an opinion.

Eventually he interrupts the meeting with: 'Sorry, but can't we move on to the next point? We're wasting time and I have to be at another meeting at 11.00.'

You feel the pace is fine for the other participants. How would you handle the situation?

HOW WOULD YOU RESPOND?

All trainers will have experienced challenges and interventions similar to the ones described here.

As a brief test, take a little time to think how you would respond in each case. Then, as you use the book, you can identify each of the types and see how closely the techniques suggested match your own.

If in any doubt, see page 94 for the names of these four types.

No such thing as a difficult participant

NO SUCH THING AS A DIFFICULT PARTICIPANT

THE HELICOPTER PARABLE

I once knew a trainer who had to run a lot of courses and lead a lot of meetings. One day, she was running a seminar at a fine hotel in the country. The hotel had wonderful facilities: tennis courts, a swimming pool - even a helicopter landing pad!

Because of some private problems as well as some last minute bad news about cuts to her training budget, she started the meeting in a bad mood. What a morning! It seemed to the trainer that she was surrounded by a group of negative, aggressive participants. Two of the group started by disagreeing with the seminar outline. Then one of them began to complain that he'd been sent by his boss and didn't want to be there. Another was whispering to his neighbour all morning. Yet another kept interrupting to say how much more she had enjoyed a previous course on the same subject. To cap it all, one highly-qualified participant, who was usually supportive, started to criticise the way she was running the session.

At noon the trainer was dispirited. She stopped the meeting early and told the group to have a long lunch break and meet again at 15.00 - hopefully in a more positive frame of mind. As she sipped a stiff pre-lunch drink at the bar, she got talking to a man who told her he was a helicopter pilot who had flown a company president into the hotel for a conference. The two got on very well and the pilot seemed to understand the trainer's problem.

NO SUCH THING AS A DIFFICULT PARTICIPANT

THE HELICOPTER PARABLE

After about half-an-hour the pilot, who had been listening carefully, suddenly said:
'Come on, I'll take you for a flight in the helicopter!'
'What about my lunch?', moaned the trainer.
'We'll only be gone about 10 minutes', laughed the pilot.

As the helicopter lifted gently from the ground and the hotel buildings grew smaller beneath them, a very strange thing happened.

The trainer looked down at the ever-wider view of the village, then the surrounding fields and then the whole area. It was like a map spread below her and a great weight was lifted from her mind.

Her nerves relaxed and her stomach stopped hurting. She saw the conference centre. She noticed the tiny, ant-like figures and suddenly realised that these tiny dots were her group walking round the hotel grounds before lunch. But at the same time she saw fields and hills, towns and villages and sky. A vast expanse of sky. The hotel now looked small and insignificant. So unimportant. Her group was a minuscule pin-point disappearing into the distance. Everything seemed to take on a new perspective. She looked out of the pilot's side of the helicopter. There, stretching for kilometre after kilometre were forests, hills and rivers. No sign of the hotel and all her worries.

NO SUCH THING AS A DIFFICULT PARTICIPANT

THE HELICOPTER PARABLE

For the first time in the day she felt relaxed and realised that there was much more to the world and to life than just one seminar!

Funnily enough, the afternoon session went very well. Every time someone interrupted or seemed aggressive, the trainer took it very calmly. In fact she imagined she was still up in the helicopter looking down. She immediately saw how the interruption was just a very small part of the bigger picture which was her life and her job - and she smiled.

She detached herself from the arguments. She listened carefully and tried to understand why certain people were feeling hurt, embarrassed or frustrated. She sympathised with them and didn't keep worrying about time. Gradually things got smoother until, at 18.30, she was able to summarise and get the participants all to agree on action items to be transferred back to their jobs.

During cocktails that evening, another strange thing happened. The participant who had criticised her style that morning drew her aside and said: 'The afternoon session went well, didn't it? But I've been talking to the group and we can't understand why you were such a difficult course leader this morning.'

'Me, a difficult course leader?' thought the trainer. 'Mmmm, and I thought they were difficult participants!'

NO SUCH THING AS A DIFFICULT PARTICIPANT

OH YES THERE IS!

We can all accept the 'helicopter' story as being very wise and applicable and yet we **still** find some participants difficult!

Why is this?

However relaxed, self-confident and serene we are, challengers make us feel inadequate in two ways:

- They make us aware of our limitations

- They give us a fear of losing control and not being able to handle the situation, a person, the group or, indeed, ourselves

WHY TECHNIQUES AND TACTICS?

If there is no such thing as a difficult participant, how come this book is about how to deal with them?

- The magic days when challenges just melt away in the warmth of your serenity are few and far between. The techniques and tactics described in this book will help you on the other days!

- Even if your mind-set is totally participant oriented, the energy displaced by challengers needs channelling so as to allow as many participants as possible to meet their objectives. These techniques and tactics are ways of channelling that energy

FOLLOW THE FEAR

Paradoxically, the best way to deal with the sudden flow of adrenalin brought on by a threatening remark from a participant is to move forward - to follow the fear, not back away from it.

- In skiing or windsurfing, as soon as we feel threatened, we instinctively hug the slope or lean *in* instead of relaxing and leaning *out* towards the perceived danger

- When driving, we instinctively brake when coming into a corner instead of gently accelerating out of it. And so it is with challengers

We should use open, relaxed body language and move towards the challenger both mentally and physically. This positive response will almost always calm things down and help you get up in that helicopter!

NO SUCH THING AS A DIFFICULT PARTICIPANT

SELF-FULFILLING PROPHECIES

In behavioural situations like training courses and meetings, people often behave according to our predictions.

We expect them to behave in a certain way and we therefore treat them accordingly. This treatment often encourages them to adopt the expected behaviour. It's what we call a 'self-fulfilling prophecy'.

The opposite is also true! If we refuse to accept the idea that a challenger is 'difficult', we will treat them with respect and understanding, expecting them to react accordingly. And nine times out of ten they do.

NO SUCH THING AS A DIFFICULT PARTICIPANT

IS IT ME? (TEST)

Think back to the last course where one or several participants gave you a hard time.
Put yourself in their shoes. Which of the following phrases might describe why they
found you a difficult trainer?

CHECKLIST/TEST

- I was prejudiced ☐
- I was too directive ☐
- I was too sure of myself ☐
- I didn't practise what I preached ☐
- I didn't keep my promises (time, etc) ☐
- I was too impatient ☐
- I didn't show how to apply knowledge ☐
- I acted as if they were... ☐
- I didn't make them feel involved ☐
- I didn't allay their fears ☐

- I was too young/inexperienced ☐
- I was too old and out of touch ☐
- I made them feel insecure ☐
- I changed their places! ☐
- I cut short their breaks ☐
- I was too 'unstructured'/free-wheeling ☐
- I forgot their names ☐
- I was too 'touchy feely' ☐
- I was too theoretical ☐

IS IT THE COURSE? (TEST)

Think back to the last course where one or several participants gave you a hard time. Which of the following phrases might describe why they found the experience difficult?

CHECKLIST/TEST

- Inadequate introduction ☐
- No icebreaker/inclusion activity ☐
- No contract/no rules ☐
- No link to the job ☐
- Unannounced/bad role play ☐
- Too theoretical ☐
- No access to telephones ☐
- There were 'outsiders' present ☐

- The boss was present ☐
- Exercises were badly designed ☐
- Equipment didn't work ☐
- Unprofessional organisation ☐
- No needs analysis ☐
- Forced to come by boss ☐
- Didn't know why they were there ☐
- Misunderstanding on timetable ☐

THE CHALLENGERS

On the next 48 pages you will find descriptions of 24 different kinds of challenging participant, along with several suggestions about how to handle them. Each challenger is allocated two pages which are divided as follows:

1) **NAME OF CHALLENGER**
2) ● Characteristics, symptoms, behaviours
3) **Suggested Intervention Technique/Tactics**

A full description of each of the techniques is contained in the final chapter.

CHALLENGERS

AGGRESSIVE/DEFENSIVE

Profile

- Interprets every new idea as a personal attack on his/her present behaviour or lack of knowledge
- Questions all assignments as to their usefulness and applicability
- Refuses to participate in role plays or exercises (especially video)

Naming

Paradoxically, naming sensitive people in examples to some extent allays their fears. When you are introducing a new system and say something like: 'Let's imagine that Janet has just started using the new system in her department and has a problem with .....', you pre-empt Janet's own reservations. She won't have to protest how unfair or difficult the new system is going to be for her - you protested for her!

CHALLENGERS

AGGRESSIVE/DEFENSIVE

Psychological Judo
Hypersensitive participants are easy to identify quickly. Think ahead to assignments such as role plays and prepare for a possible refusal with some psychological judo. For instance: 'This afternoon we'll be doing some simple role plays (explain the details). We've obviously done these exercises many times before, but if there's anyone who feels they cannot help their colleagues in this way and does not wish to participate, please let me know during the break, we will fully understand.' When approached by the hypersensitive one, emphasise the safe nature of the exercise but encourage them not to participate. Human nature is such that they'll probably change their mind during lunch.

NB Your own sensitivity is vital here. Some people are indeed so sensitive that any up-front performance can mortify them and paralyse learning. Act accordingly and protect them in the most appropriate way.

THE DINOSAUR

Profile
- Demonstrates an unwillingness to question own beliefs
- Makes 'black and white', 'right and wrong' statements
- Displays clear prejudices and rigid opinions
- Voices discomfort with abstract and/or 'new age' thinking

Agree/Disagree/Deflect
Find something about their intervention with which to agree but then gently disagree on the main issues. Example: 'I agree....but I'm not sure I can agree with you on XYZ.' Then deflect: 'How do the rest of you feel about this?'

Reflect/Deflect
Say something like: 'So you're really saying that there's nothing wrong with the old way of doing things?' Depending on their rephrasing of their intervention, deflect to the group or an individual for comment.

THE DINOSAUR

Confrontation Show respect for and accept their feelings and value system but make it clear that the purpose of the course is to challenge the present way of thinking. Ask permission to allow 'crazier' participants to say their piece.

3rd Person Persuasion Find or invent an appropriate anecdote, metaphor or parable about a person (or perhaps a dinosaur!) who didn't want to change and the consequences. This technique is most powerful when used in a non-specific way. In other words, choose an appropriate moment (like the beginning or the end of a session) and address all the participants - don't pick on the dinosaur. Let the message get to each of them in its own way.

Reframe (Helicopter) Listen carefully to their interventions. Say something like: 'I can understand how it looks from your point of view. Let me just tell you how it looks from my point of view - then perhaps we can agree to disagree.'

Psychological Judo Ask them to be the 'protector of the faith' and to interrupt whenever they feel you are going too far and misleading the other participants with unrealistic or unethical suggestions.

THE DOODLER

Profile
- Makes more or less elaborate drawings on notepaper while you are talking

Ignore!
It's probably a sign of concentration. Doodlers can often listen much more attentively when not distracted by the body language of the trainer.
The doodle is an unconscious representation of their thought processes as they listen and absorb.

THE DOODLER

Naming

If the doodling bothers you try using the doodler's name in an example, or ask them an open question to get involvement. This will allow you to check whether they are following. If so, ignore doodling!

Refocus

Use an overhead transparency or the flip chart to divert their attention away from the doodling.

Psychological Judo

In a meeting you could ask the doodler to capture the essence of each module or agenda item as a concise drawing on an overhead transparency to be shown at the end of the meeting.

CHALLENGERS

THE EAGER BEAVER

Profile

- Keeps trying to help but interventions do more harm than good
- Nods and smiles but is an 'own goal scorer' whose contributions miss the point
- Embarrasses team members by gleefully interrupting trainer with interpretations of their discussions

Reframe (Relevance)

Ask them (nicely!) to explain the relevance of their remarks. Say something like: 'Sorry, but help me to see how this fits in with what we've been discussing.' Try and channel the response back to the subject, with thanks.
If this doesn't work .....

THE EAGER BEAVER

Reframe (Helicopter)

Say something like: 'I can see how you experienced XYZ from the perspective of an ABC, but let's ask someone else to what extent they also see it from that angle.'

Then:

Deflect

To group or individual: 'Anyone?' 'Bridget?' If the eager beaver keeps causing a problem try .....

You and Me

- Make it clear verbally or non-verbally that you know that they are trying to help, but that you want to hear from the others

- Speak to them during a break and ask for their help in letting the others express themselves

THE EXHIBITIONIST

Profile
- Asks embarrassing questions about his/her personal situation
- Indulges in extreme self-revelation
- Embarrasses others with his/her candour
- Washes dirty linen in public
- Always ready with: 'I remember once when I .....'

Action Reply
Use the interventions as instant case study opportunities for other participants to discuss their opinions on a course-related subject and then refocus.

Example:
During an in-company training course on assertiveness a female 'exhibitionist' asks the following question: 'You know there's this man in the office - I can't tell you who it is obviously - who keeps pestering me to go out with him. Actually he's quite sexy so I wouldn't mind but, well.... I mean, how can I say 'no' and still stay, you know, good friends?'

THE EXHIBITIONIST

What the trainer could do is to say:

'Thanks for your candour. Let's not go into too many details here but you've raised a very powerful question. How can we say 'no' to people without losing their esteem. John, how could you say 'no' to your boss on some unwanted overtime?'

Refocus

Another way would be to refocus by asking the group: 'How would this personal experience fit in with the theory we were discussing earlier?'

Confrontation

Point out sincerely and in a straightforward way that their behaviour is out of order. Explain that the course was not designed as a personal therapy and/or exorcism session. Try and do this with humour!

CHALLENGERS

THE EXPERT

Profile
- Wants to be recognised as the expert; wants the spotlight
- Knows as much as you - if not more!
- Interrupts to point out mistakes or to disagree with facts
- Tells stories, gives examples to demonstrate expertise

Receipt
Always thank or give receipt for contributions.

Blockbusting
Ask for specifics. Refer to person's own words and ask for details which will reinforce your message.

CHALLENGERS

THE EXPERT

Reflect/Deflect

After a question (which is really a request for the spotlight) say: 'What you're asking is ..?' When they rephrase, say: 'You've obviously thought a lot about it, what do you think?' and deflect the answer back to them.

Psychological Judo

- Ask for help/advice and treat as 'co-leader'

- Give special tasks such as 'truth watchdog' (or, as some trainers call it, 'bullshit monitor') to help you ensure that facts are correct. Other tasks could be 'scribe' - to keep notes (and keep them quiet!) - or 'summariser' to make regular recaps on what has been covered

- Consult during breaks as confidential 'assistant'

- If interventions are too frequent and disruptive, ask for help with a really difficult question. Their inability to answer may make them think twice before interrupting again

CHALLENGERS

THE GRIPER

Profile
- Is fatalistically negative when questioned
- Shrugs shoulders
- Complains about everything
- Didn't want to come in the first place
- Whinges when asked to do anything

Reflect/Deflect
Provoke by reflecting a strong negative resumé of their interventions.

Example: 'So you're saying that there's no way this can possibly work in our organisation.'

However much the griper then dilutes the original gripe, deflect the strong version to the group: 'Do we all agree that this is doomed to failure?' Nine times out of ten the positive thinkers will rally round you to sanction the griper. If more than 50% of the group agrees with the griper then you have a mutiny! See **Mutineers.**

THE GRIPER

Reframe (Consequences)

Ask a question such as: 'You obviously can't go on working in an environment which is so painful for you. How do you suggest we handle the rest of this course .....?'

Psychological Judo

Ask them to be the official 'devil's advocate' whose job is to note down why the various topics you cover won't work, and any other negative things triggered by the course content. Whenever they attempt to speak, signal them to note down their thoughts in the interests of time. During a break go through their list and add a couple of your own 'moans'. Ask them to make a short 'devil's advocate' presentation. They'll either be a complete flop and self-correct out of embarrassment or provide you with some useful and objective counter-arguments.

THE HIJACKER

Profile
- Wants to take over
- Suggests that the time available would be spent more usefully on another subject
- Asks questions which lead you away from the course topic
- Tries to get a personal work problem resolved during course

Refocus
- Thank them for observations
- Remind them of topic
- Use overhead transparency or flip chart to refocus attention. If this does not work .....

Reflect/Deflect
Say something like: 'If I understand you correctly, you think we should drop this part of the programme and work on XYZ. How do the rest of you feel?'

THE HIJACKER

Nine times out of ten the majority of the group will 'subdue' the hijacker and you can get on with the course.

In a rare case where over 50% of the group agree with the hijacker, then you have a mutiny. See **Mutineers** for how to handle this.

Psychological Judo

- Ask for their help to change the course structure or meeting agenda to better address the needs of all participants. Keep checking back with others for agreement. If they don't agree, encourage them to subdue the hijacker
- As with a real hijacker, keep them busy with questions, requests for help, discussion, etc until they give up and can be readily subdued. Then REFOCUS (with overhead transparency or flip chart or simply a change of tone) and move on

THE JOKER

Profile
- Tells jokes/funny stories
- Makes fun of serious topics
- Makes (vulgar) innuendoes
- Never misses a pun
- Mocks other participants

Building
If other participants are enjoying it, use your own humorous repartee to build on the humour. Don't try and stifle it - use it.

Confrontation
If others are offended, confront the joker during the break and explain that others are sensitive. Ask him/her for an effort.

THE JOKER

Non-verbal
Show your enjoyment or distaste with exaggerated grimaces and gestures.

Action Reply
After a few inappropriate 'humorous' interventions, choose a serious point and ask another participant how they think the joker would make a joke out of it.

Psychogical Judo
First, enjoy all humorous interventions, then ask for help. Point out that humour is essential to learning and attention (right brain function) and ask the joker for periodic humorous resumés of the course. You might even ask them to invent a joke about other participants. Since it's difficult and offensive, they will usually refrain!

THE MUTINEERS

Profile

- This special category of challenger applies to a group of over 50% of participants at a course, meeting or presentation who agree with a trouble-maker, griper or hijacker

Adjourn!

Stop the course and re-schedule.

Change the Programme/Agenda

Submit to the participants that, in view of the 'mutiny', the agenda should be changed to deal with the problem. If it's serious enough they will agree and you can get SOMETHING done.

CHALLENGERS

THE MUTINEERS

Reframe (Consequences)
Get them to see how their 'mutiny', although understandable, must be logically justified (put your money where your mouth is!). Examples:

1. You could get them to help you draw up a list of logical reasons why XYZ won't work and ask one of them to present it to management.

2. State that you understand how difficult it must be for them to be working in such a bad/demotivating environment. Suggest that they use the course learning for their NEXT job!

NB Psychologically, when participants start to agree with a negative colleague, they let off steam and tend to escalate the gripes and moans BEYOND their real feelings. They exaggerate their grievances. A skilled facilitator knows this and remains calm. By clever reframing, you can usually bring things back on track and get participants to self-correct. Once they've vented their feelings they will very often stop complaining and start to find reasonable compromises.

THE PART-TIMER

Profile
- Arrives late, leaves early
- Announces that s/he will miss complete sessions because of 'prior commitments'
- Gets called away to important meetings

Confrontation
As soon as you feel that his/her absenteeism is becoming or will become an issue, confront during a break. Depending on the situation:
- Explain why full attendance is important – maybe to the extent of suggesting exclusion from the course

CHALLENGERS

THE PART-TIMER

Confrontation – cont'd
- Point out how unfair the absences are for other participants
  (ie in exercises and group work)
- Suggest that you talk to his/her boss about signing up for a future session of the course when things are less hectic on the job
- If the course finishes with the awarding of a certificate, inform them as soon as possible that this requires full attendance

Refocus
Give the part-timer an important role in a team for exercises where their full attendance is required – in plenary sessions to understand the issues and in group work to ensure task completion.

Reflect/Deflect (in the part-timer's breakout group)
Having spoken to the part-timer about their forthcoming disappearance(s), explain the situation to the group and ask them to decide how to deal with the absence. You could even ask them how fair they think this coming and going is and what to do about it .

THE REFEREE/PEDANT

Profile
- Wants to follow rules - even to the detriment of efficiency
- Interrupts to quibble over details
- Points out spelling mistakes on slides
- Exasperates other participants with pedantic and long-winded analyses/explanations

Self-revelation
Apologise for your errors, explaining that it's not one of your strong points, thank and quickly move on.

3rd Person Persuasion
Tell an anecdote, metaphor or parable (without specifying who you're talking about or why) which illustrates the need for flexibility. For example, you could stress the need for everybody to keep an open mind, and tell a parable about a war hero who got a medal because he disobeyed the rules.

THE REFEREE/PEDANT

Agree/Disagree
First agree with their interruption and thank them, but then point out that you'd like to ask for a little flexibility so that the whole group can benefit from the course.

Psychological Judo
Ask them to be the group 'auditor' or 'referee'. Explain how difficult it is for you to lead the course and at the same time ensure discipline. Request that they ensure everyone (including you) sticks to the rules. Give them a whistle or yellow card to use every time anyone transgresses. (They'll very soon get fed up with this official role.)

THE RIVALS

Profile
- Two representatives of different departments or different schools of thought who use the course to 'get at' each other
- Make humorous, sarcastic or even aggressive put-downs of each other
- Use course material as ammunition against one another

Confrontation
Ask them to keep their rivalry for outside the training room in the interests of other participants.

CHALLENGERS

THE RIVALS

Psychological Judo
Institutionalise their rivalry. Appoint each to the head of a team. Create exercises where they can compete. Ask each to make a presentation of their group findings. (This will channel their competitive energy toward the course topics and not 'back-on-the job' problems.)

Reflect/Deflect
Address both of them and say something like: 'If I understand correctly, you'd like to use this course as a duelling ground and try and score points off each other?' Wait for reply, then deflect: 'How does the rest of the group feel about this situation?'

Refocus
Give each an absorbing role/task within their group (example: scribe, facilitator, in charge of the recap session) to use up their spare 'duelling' energy.

CHALLENGERS

THE SHOW-OFF

Profile

- Feels undervalued, seeks spotlight to 'prove' himself/herself to others
- Not interested in helping you, only in impressing the others
- Puts you down in order to score points
- Monopolises discussions
- Alienates other participants

Blockbusting

Ask for specifics. Refer to their own words and ask for details which will support/reinforce your message.

THE SHOW-OFF

Reflect/Deflect

Give a chance to the group or an individual to censor them. Example from a team meeting:

'Great! It sounds like you've had a lot of experience in this area. Right?' (Wait for falsely modest reply and deflect to group with a smile). 'Anyone like to challenge X's expertise on this one?'

Or deflect to an individual/expert: 'Bill, would you agree with X's position on this one?'

Psychological Judo

- Ask for a mini-presentation on a difficult subject in front of the group. Encourage showing off until they realise they will make a fool of themselves by continuing

- Ask for help with a very difficult question in an area in which you know they are weak

- Give them a special task to occupy their attention and provide the spotlight. (See also **The Expert**.)

CHALLENGERS

THE SHY VIOLET

Profile
- Avoids eye contact
- Blushes easily
- Speaks rarely and in a quiet voice
- Never volunteers information

Building
Build on their rare contributions.
For example: 'Yes, that's absolutely right and you'll also find that .....'

Questions
Ask easy closed questions to boost their ego.
Show appreciation for the right answer.

THE SHY VIOLET

Naming
Use their names in examples and metaphors to boost their confidence: 'Let's imagine that Rick and Jennifer had a problem with the warehouse team .....'

Psychological Judo
(Rarely necessary but extremely powerful.)
Prescribe the 'silent' symptoms by asking them to remain quiet - but make it relatively unattractive to do so. Wait until after a break and address the whole group. Say something like: 'You all noticed before the break that this is a very open course and I'd like to hear from everybody. However, I realise that some people who are shy and timid don't like to speak in front of their colleagues. This is perfectly OK and I understand their feelings. So if you feel you'd rather not contribute because you're shy that's fine.' (Look at an open, more talkative participant). 'There are several other people who'll compensate by giving us their opinions loud and clear!' You'll find that the first person to intervene is one of the shy violets!

CHALLENGERS

THE SILENT CYNIC

Profile
- Demonstrates bored body language (reads, fiddles, looks around constantly, fidgets)
- Rolls eyes and exhales following your or other participants' affirmatives

Reflect/Deflect
Say something like: 'You don't seem to fully agree with ABC ...?'
Or: 'You seem to have some doubt about this one ...?'
Let them answer.* Then deflect to one or all of the participants.
'Would anyone (Harry?) like to disagree with X on this?'
This will give you time to think of your own
counter-arguments to add.

*It is important to make them verbalise their
disagreement or cynicism.

CHALLENGERS

THE SILENT CYNIC

Confrontation
Point out that the objective of the course is to discuss openly, and move towards a positive outcome. If the cynic isn't willing to co-operate ask him/her to leave.

Psychological Judo
Appoint as class 'cynic' (explain the original Greek meaning: contempt for ease and pleasure. One who doubts human sincerity and merit). Ask for regular, well-reasoned refutations of your or other participants' arguments to ensure that 'we don't just accept things automatically'. Generally speaking the less opposition cynics receive the more they will rally to the cause.

Reframing (Consequences)
As with the Griper ask a reframing question like: 'You obviously find it painful working in this environment. How would you handle this unnecessary course?' Then deflect suggestions to the group.

THE SLOWCOACH

Profile
- Keeps getting it wrong!
- Consistently volunteers remarks and asks questions which show he/she hasn't understood what's been happening
- Answers questions incorrectly

After *remarks* which demonstrate lack of understanding:

Reframe (Relevance)
Try and adopt the mind-set that you have done a bad job of explaining (difficult!) and say something like: 'Help me to see how what you're saying fits in with what we've been discussing?' Try and channel the response back to the subject, with thanks.

THE SLOWCOACH

After *questions* which demonstrate lack of understanding:

Deflect
Accept the question with patience and ask the group: 'Is there anyone else who feels we need to clarify this important point we discussed earlier?'

If there is, then take the time to go over the point. If not, then suggest kindly and diplomatically to the slowcoach that you have a chat over a break or lunch to recap.

Confrontation
During a break state honestly that you feel they are dropping behind the other participants (quite often it's because they have less experience or a different educational background from the others) and ask what they suggest. If no solution is forthcoming, propose that they either *stay* but not slow down the others with remarks or questions, or *leave* with the justification that they were wrongly selected to attend.

THE SPEEDY GONZALEZ

Profile
- Finishes exercises and assignments well before others
- Is always one step ahead when asking questions; is impatient with slower participants
- Asks to move on before you are ready

Confrontation
Ask for patience and explain in a positive way why others need more time (learning styles, experience, etc).

3rd Person Persuasion
Find or invent an appropriate parable/metaphor to tell at the beginning or end of a session. For example: the tortoise and the hare, or a metaphorical version of it which applies to the course subject matter. This could be a story in praise of thorough preparation or about the dangers of jumping to conclusions. As always, address the metaphor/parable to the whole group in the guise of a general teaching point. Allow the message to get to each participant in its own way.

CHALLENGERS

THE SPEEDY GONZALEZ

Psychological Judo
- Appoint as co-leader/scribe/summariser
- Give them a complex task to finish quickly
- Ask very difficult questions to slow them down
- Ask them to find real examples of what you're saying - especially when none has been volunteered
- Give them two exercises/assignments to do instead of one and keep highlighting how brilliant/fast/intelligent they are

(Even the speediest Gonzalez starts to retreat under a spotlight as hot as this!)

THE STARMAKER

Profile
- Is your number one fan!
- Nods, smiles, agrees with everything you say
- Gives examples to others of your brilliance
- Makes others feel uncomfortable with his/her oozing support of your arguments

Self-revelation
State honestly that this (hero-worship) embarrasses you.

THE STARMAKER

Confrontation
During a break let them know how much you appreciate their support but ask them to be less loquacious about it. Explain that you don't wish to influence the other participants unfairly, but let them make up their own minds - just as the Starmaker has done!

Action Reply
Following a particularly glowing endorsement of something you have said, thank them for their support and say: 'Mr X is obviously totally in favour of XYZ. But let's play 'devil's advocate' for a moment. For the sake of objectivity, who'd like to put forward a counter-argument/express a different opinion?'

Psychological Judo
Appoint to a special job like scribe, social secretary, 'example-giver', etc in order to direct their energy.

CHALLENGERS

THE TRAPPER

Profile
- Seems to be waiting to trap you
- Jumps in to demonstrate that you are prejudiced or unprofessional
- Points out inconsistencies in your arguments/approach/examples

Self-revelation
Apologise immediately and thank the trapper for identifying the 'problem' and then:

Refocus
With an overhead transparency or flip chart.

THE TRAPPER

Naming

Refer to the trapper's previous remarks as examples of perspicacity or vigilance to emphasise the importance of their role and demonstrate your lack of defensiveness. *(Don't be sarcastic. If you can't be sincere with this technique - don't use it.)*

Reflect/Deflect

Say something like: 'You feel I have been inconsistent about ..' or: 'You seem to perceive me as a... (sexist, racist, shallow thinker, etc).' Wait for a climb down or, at least, a specification of the trapper's real intentions, then deflect to the group, or an individual: 'Does anyone else have a problem with my .....?'

Psychological Judo

Ask the trapper to be the 'watchdog' and ensure that any inconsistency or flaw is pounced upon immediately. Ask specifically for critique when none is forthcoming. Put pressure on them to find fault so that they relinquish the trapper role. Example: 'Mr Trapper, you had some useful comments about ABC just now. Do you think we've been fair/logical/realistic on *this* one?'

THE TROUBLE-MAKER

Profile
- Wants attention - even if it's negative
- Makes remarks which are aggressive or insulting
- Asks questions rudely
- Expresses a negative attitude with hostility towards you, the meeting or other participants
- Disagrees loudly and offensively with you or others

Reflect/Deflect
Interpret what you think you have heard and deflect a strong version to the group so that they will disagree and sanction the trouble-maker. (If on rare occasions the group agrees then you have a mutiny.
See page 39 for how to reframe **Mutineers**.)

CHALLENGERS

THE TROUBLE-MAKER

Reframe (Consequences) Demonstrate the consequences of the outburst. Say something like: 'You obviously have very strong feelings about this. This must also mean that you think/feel...' Reframe consequences of the negative/aggressive attitude until trouble-maker retreats.

Reframe (Table-turn) Use trouble-maker's own arguments against him/her. Example:

TROUBLE-MAKER: 'This is ridiculous! We simply don't have time to do all this.'
YOU: 'I understand. But don't forget it's not compulsory. It's optional to be a professional in your job.'

Psychological Judo Ask for a big favour to channel negative energy into something positive. For example, you could ask them to work the camera or lead a small group feedback session during a video role play exercise. Appoint them as 'devil's advocate' to intervene whenever they feel you're leading the group astray. Applaud their courage in standing up for their opinions and constantly ask them for negative comments so as to get both sides of the argument out in the open.

(When the spotlight gets too hot even trouble-makers melt!)

(61)

THE WHISPERER

Profile
- Makes whispered comments to neighbour

NB There is only one whisperer - the other is the whisperee! In many cases the whisperee is an unwilling accomplice so you only have one person to handle.

Refocus
Use a slide or the flip chart to attract and refocus their attention.

DO NOT SAY: 'Would you like to share your interesting conversation with everyone?' It's sarcastic and directive and likely to cause resentment.

THE WHISPERER

Non-verbal

To use this technique effectively you must always assume that the whisperers are enthusiastically building on something you said – even if they're not!

1. Stop talking and look *unthreateningly* at them.
2. Wait for them to look at you.
3. *Non-verbally* ask for their permission to continue (eyebrows raised, head-nod and perhaps a silent-mouthed 'OK?').

The sincerity and vulnerability projected by your positive mind-set is normally guaranteed to provoke a spontaneous sharing of the whispered message. It will also encourage whisperers to self-control in future.

Psychological Judo

Wait until after a break. Explain that you have a lot of ground to cover in the forthcoming session. Invite anyone who has any difficulty in keeping up (getting old or having trouble understanding) to ask their neighbour. Say, with a smile, that you don't mind them whispering to each other as long as they are discreet!

CHALLENGERS

THE WOOLLY THINKER

Profile
- Makes vague, abstract contributions
- Asks rambling unclear questions

Self-revelation
When asked an unclear question, say something like:
'I'm sorry but I'm not sure I understood your point there.
You feel that .....?'

Blockbusting
Ask for clarification of contributions with 'which, what,
when and who ... specifically?' questions.

THE WOOLLY THINKER

Reflect/Deflect

After vague questions or contributions make a purposefully more specific interpretation of what you think they meant. For example:

1. WOOLLY THINKER: 'Well, it's all a question of motivation really.'
   YOU: 'So what you're saying is that you find it demotivating working in that department?'
   WT: 'No, no. Not me! No, I just think the office staff need to feel more motivated about doing the routine work.'
   YOU: 'Does anyone else have examples of demotivated office staff?'

2. WT: 'I think it's a communication problem.'
   YOU: 'Your boss doesn't talk to you?'
   WT: 'Oh yes, don't get me wrong. No, there's just too much crap on the email every morning.'
   YOU: Fred, you were complaining about email the other day, what do you think?

THE YAWNER/SLEEPER

Profile

Phase 1:
- Yawns
- Stifles yawns
- Eyelids droop

Phase 2:
- Closes eyes and seems to be (is) sleeping!

Naming

Use their name in examples and metaphors without looking at them. For example: 'Let's imagine that Miss Y was one of our customers .....' Get a discussion going with the rest of the group. Once she's had a chance to 'wake up', catch her eye and say something like: 'In a moment I'll ask Miss Y, our customer, how she would feel about what we're saying.'

THE YAWNER/SLEEPER

Non-verbal
In one of her 'open-eyelid' moments catch her eye and nod/wink or give some other signal to indicate that you know she's dropping off but won't show her up in front of the others.

Confrontation (use with care!)
Address the problem openly. Say something like: 'Mr X obviously had a hard night last night and is having a tough time keeping awake. How can we help him?' If you do it in a good humoured way, the adrenalin rush caused by the embarrassment will usually help them over the 'low'. (Think of when it's happened to you!)

Call a Break
Allow the sleeper and the others to get some fresh air.

Psychological Judo
(To use when showing videos in the afternoon, for example)
Say something like: 'Now is the ideal time for anyone over 35 who needs a rest after lunch, to have a quick shut-eye. The rest of us are going to watch this excellent film!' You'll notice how the older ones go out of their way to show how much they enjoyed the video!

NOTES

TECHNIQUES AND TACTICS

TECHNIQUES AND TACTICS

IT'S THEIR COURSE

On the following pages are full descriptions of each of the intervention techniques/tactics mentioned in the Challengers section.

Please remember that there are no 'difficult' participants!

- It's *their* course or meeting
- Challengers are much less disruptive when the trainer/leader is non-defensive and serene
- Intervention techniques are necessary *only* to:
  - optimise resources and get to learning/consensus faster and with less energy;
  - allay the trainer's fears of losing control of the group

TECHNIQUES AND TACTICS

ACTION REPLY

As with action REPLAYS on television, this is a 'one more time' technique.

When faced with certain challenging interventions, you use the question or remark as an opportunity for a practical exercise - especially if there is no easy answer.

- Organise an instant role play or case study

Example:
'Mmm, that's an interesting question. Let's try and act this one out. Why don't you (challenger) play the role of X and you (another participant) the role of Y and let's see how it goes?'

- Break into discussion groups to debate the topic
- Create a plenary case study out of the question

AGREE/DISAGREE/DEFLECT

When you disagree with a participant's remarks or arguments but don't wish to embarrass them, first:

● Find SOMETHING about the contribution with which to agree

Then:

● Gently disagree with the key issue

Lastly:

● Deflect to the group for comment

Example:

'Yes, you are absolutely right that this situation is extremely common. I'm not sure that this is the only way to handle it however. Has anyone else found another way to deal with it?'

BLOCKBUSTING

Asking closed, specific questions to cut through vague or abstract contributions. Use participant's OWN words.

- Which, when, where, what, who.... specifically?
- How many, how far, how often, how old, how soon.... exactly?
- Everybody? Always? None? All of them? Etc.
- Compared to what? (Following a vague generalisation)
- What are you using as evidence?

Example:

Participant:	'Well, it's a question of bad communication really, isn't it?'
Leader:	'Sorry, which bad communication exactly?'
Participant:	'Well, people don't talk to each other, do they?'
Leader:	'I know what you mean, but what are you using as evidence that people don't talk to each other?'
Participant:	'Well, only the other day....'

BUILDING

Quite simply BUILDING on what a participant has said by adding something to show how their contribution fits into the construction of the learning point.

Example:	
Participant:	'I think it's important to praise people when they perform well. It motivates them.'
Leader:	'Absolutely! That's one of the guiding principles of our system. And when people are motivated they are much more open to bear constructive criticism - to discuss how they can improve.'

CONFRONTATION

Sometimes, the best way to handle a challenger is to go straight to the point and address the unwanted behaviour.

> **Examples**:
> - 'Could I ask you to abide by the no evaluation of ideas rule until we get to the next step?'
> - 'Sorry to interrupt you, Fred, but could we hear from someone from the sales department on this one?'

More usually, confrontation is a last resort technique to be used one-on-one during a break. Take the challenger to one side and specify simply and honestly the behaviour you wish him/her to change. Always look for a pay-off for them if they do change, but accept that the only solution may be for them to leave the course or meeting.

TECHNIQUES AND TACTICS

NAMING

This is perhaps the most powerful technique for keeping participants' attention and interest – but it needs mental agility and a good memory. There are basically two kinds of naming:

Backtrack Naming
Refer to participants' names and to contributions they made earlier. For example: 'Sandy mentioned a similar incident yesterday and Joe told us about how *he* handled a case.'

Example/Metaphor Naming
Use participants' names in your illustrations and metaphors. For example: 'Let's imagine that Jessica wanted to key into this programme, how would she start?'

Naming is particularly useful for:

- Boosting participants' confidence
- Pre-empting objections
- Giving the spotlight to those who want it
- Keeping boredom at bay

NON-VERBAL

When 'words fail you' a non-verbal signal can be very effective in handling participant interventions.

> **Examples**:
> - Hands up in mock surrender
> - Hands over ears as if it's all too much
> - Sideways glance to other participants as if to say: 'We've got a right one here'
> - A culturally acceptable 'my foot' gesture or mime
> - A mock and exaggerated frown to show surprised disagreement (but 'please convince me I'm wrong!')
> - Eyebrows raised in mock surprise/horror

TECHNIQUES AND TACTICS

PSYCHOLOGICAL JUDO

When faced with challenging behaviour you 'prescribe the symptoms' of that behaviour. In other words you ask for MORE of the unhelpful behaviour but, at the same time, you make it unattractive for the participant to continue. As in judo, when the barrier against which the participant is pushing is taken away, they suddenly feel out in the open and vulnerable and will direct their attacking energy on to something more helpful.

> **Example**:
> When a smoker is given a whistle to blow every time they feel you should interrupt the course for their right to a smoke break, they rarely blow the whistle.
>
> They *now* wish to demonstrate their willpower.

TECHNIQUES AND TACTICS

RECEIPT

The most basic and non-negotiable of all techniques.

Simply give a receipt for EVERY contribution made by ANY participant!

- Say thank you and mention their name
- Rephrase to fit your teaching point. For example: 'OK, so you're saying that .... Good!'
- Simply repeat the last phrase and ask for other comments

TECHNIQUES AND TACTICS

REFLECT/DEFLECT

DEFINITION

Reflect/Deflect is the process name for a relatively classic method of dealing with participant challenges.

The method consists of:

- Reflecting back to the challenger what you think you have heard
- Deflecting to one, several or all of the other participants the responsibility of responding to the new, clarified version of the challenge

The technique is based on the mind-set that:

- You don't have to have all the answers
- Participants generally want you to succeed and will 'rescue' you from aggression
- It's THEIR course/meeting anyway!

TECHNIQUES AND TACTICS

REFLECT/DEFLECT

3 TYPES OF REFLECTION

1. CHERRY-PICKING
   Take part of the intervention only and reflect it back.
   - 'Let's first take your remark on XYZ. You feel that ....?'

2. INTERPRETING
   Reflect back your version of what the challenger said.
   - 'If I understand correctly, your problem/question is ....?'

3. PROVOKING
   Reflect back an even stronger version of the implied attack, criticism or 'heckle' to provoke a climb down or, at least, a diluted restatement of aggression.
   - 'So you're saying that XYZ really made you furious?' (Hoping for, 'Well, not exactly furious, but I do think ....')

TECHNIQUES AND TACTICS

REFLECT/DEFLECT
3 TYPES OF DEFLECTION

1. RETURN TO SENDER
    80% of questions and challenges are not what they appear. They are requests for the spotlight. When you feel trapped by a question, first reflect back what you think the participant was asking, then ask HIM/HER. You can then comment on their opinion or deflect to the group.

    Example:
    Participant: 'How do you think ABC's new system will affect our sales?'
    Leader: 'Ah now, do you feel it will have an impact on us pretty soon?'

2. RICOCHET
    Deflect your reflection to ONE other participant:
    *   'Alex, you work in that department, how do you feel about....?'

3. PEER PRESSURE
    Deflect your reflection to the whole group for comment:
    *   'How do the rest of you feel....?'

TECHNIQUES AND TACTICS

REFOCUS

Whenever a discussion starts to wander or when you are under pressure (from the clock or from a participant) refocus by diverting the group's attention to something else.

- Distribute a handout
- Switch on the projector/show a slide
- Go to the flip chart and write something
- (If you are seated) Get up and spread your hands out, palms down
- Use emphatic 'Right!' 'OK!'
- Find a verbal bridge or link to the next point. Interrupt the participant(s) by saying something like: 'Yes, that's important because.....' (link to next point)

With 'unfocused' individual participants, assign them a role/task that will require full attention.

REFRAMING
4 TYPES OF REFRAME

Reframing consists of cutting a
challenging intervention short by
getting the participant to consider their
remarks from a different point of view or 'frame'.

1. RELEVANCE
   Asking participants to consider the
   relevance of what they are saying to the
   point being discussed!
   - 'Help me to see how this fits in with
     what we've been discussing'

2. HELICOPTER
   Agreeing that one can look at the problem from that angle but showing them
   another view (from the other side of the helicopter).

REFRAMING

4 TYPES OF REFRAME (Cont'd)

3. TABLE-TURNING
    Turning a tricky situation to your advantage by
    reframing the premise of the challenge.

    *   Ronald Reagan, when attacked on
        his age by a journalist during the
        final debate with Mondale, said:
        'I will not make age an issue of this
        campaign. I refuse to exploit for
        political purposes my opponent's
        youth and inexperience'

    *   Churchill, when Lady Astor said: 'If
        you were my husband, I'd put
        poison in your wine', retorted:
        'Madam, if I were your husband,
        I'd drink it!'

REFRAMING

4 TYPES OF REFRAME (Cont'd)

4. CONSEQUENCES
   When participants are griping about the organisation/the boss/the course, etc reframe the consequences of what they are saying:

   - 'You are obviously very unhappy working here and I can understand why you don't think this course is relevant or applicable to your jobs. Please help me to draw up a list of reasons why you think we're wasting our time here, so I can present it to my management. We could save a lot of money!'

SELF-REVELATION

This is a technique which shouldn't be used as a technique! It should come naturally. There are two general challenging situations in which self-revelation is effective:

- When you have been criticised or attacked. For example: 'I feel hurt by that remark. I'm sorry. I don't know how to respond to that kind of criticism'

- When you need to show empathy for someone who is expressing deep feelings. For example: 'I know how you must have felt. I remember my own experience very well. It .....'

Your honesty and openness will demonstrate a vulnerability which will defuse aggression and generate warmth – as long as it doesn't become a behavioural habit.

3RD PERSON PERSUASION

DEFINITION

A series of techniques based on Milton Erikson's psychotherapy – helping a participant resolve a problem by giving an example of how a non-threatening 3rd person found a solution. This person may be real or fictitious.

The 3rd person gambit removes the threat of having to follow the teacher's advice. It makes it easier for the problem poser to turn suggestions into his/her OWN solutions without losing face.

TECHNIQUES AND TACTICS

3RD PERSON PERSUASION

1. ANECDOTES

Faced with a 'yes-butting' solution-seeker, admit that you can't help. Later, recount an anecdote which is relevant to the problem but don't overtly point out the link. Try and keep the hidden advice distant from the participant in question.

Example:
'We were talking yesterday about XYZ and it reminded me of something a friend of mine told me about one of his relations. Apparently .....'

3RD PERSON PERSUASION

2. METAPHORS

A metaphor or analogy starts with the words: 'It's a bit like.....'. When faced with a challenger who finds it difficult to accept or understand new ideas, look for a metaphor which illustrates the learning point in another way.

The power of the metaphor is that it puts left brain information into a right brain format, a bit like Apple did when they first developed their visual intuitive desktop approach to personal computing. Before that, using computers involved complex scientific systems and coding.

Example:
People who find it hard to change remind me of the old Guinness advert: 'I've never tried it because I don't like it!'

3RD PERSON PERSUASION

3. PARABLES

When you wish to persuade participants to adopt new behaviours or attitudes, a parable is sometimes the most powerful tool.

- Find or create a story like the one on pages 10-12 of this Pocketbook – introduce it a bit like a fairy tale

- Make sure you include lots of visual imagery

- Describe the central character's feelings by trying to equate them to those of the participants

- Give the parable a 'moral' which the participants' brains will have to link to what you're saying

TECHNIQUES AND TACTICS

3RD PERSON PERSUASION

4. NEIGHBOURLY PERSUASION

When faced with a challenging problem-poser, talk to one of their neighbours about how *they* would have solved a similar problem.

Insist that the solution is very probably inapplicable to the one originally stated.

NB As with all the 3rd person techniques, you should not be the one to make links – if any. The 'magic' behind the technique is that the links are made automatically (and sometimes subconsciously) in the brain of the challenger – as long as you leave them alone!

3RD PERSON PERSUASION

5. ALTERNATIVES

If you are faced with a particularly tenacious problem-poser, try brainstorming possible solutions with the whole group.

Select at least three possible alternative solutions and note keywords on a flip chart.

Insist that probably none of the suggestions will solve such a difficult problem but point out that OTHER participants might like to try them for THEIR problems.

This will allow the challenger to overcome the 'not invented here' barrier and be absolved from having to use any of them. Thus he or she will be the decision-maker as to what to do.

TECHNIQUES AND TACTICS

YOU AND ME

This technique is especially useful with frequent contributors. When faced with experts or 'know alls' who constantly interrupt (whether their contributions are relevant or not) you need to ask them to allow others to have their say.

The 'you and me' technique consists of making it clear verbally or non-verbally that YOU know they know but that you want also to hear from the other (less knowledgeable) participants.

Non-verbally this can be done with eyebrow movements, a wink, a smile and some blocking hand movements. Always try and keep the interrupter on your side. Make them feel that they are co-trainers. Hence 'you and me against the others'.

> Difficult situations
> (pages 4 - 7)
> the Challengers are:
>
> 1. Trouble-maker
> 2. Trapper
> 3. Whisperer
> 4. Speedy Gonzalez

About the Author

John Townsend, BA MA MCIPD
John has built a reputation internationally as a leading trainer of trainers.
He is the founder of the highly-regarded Master Trainer Institute, a total
learning facility located just outside Geneva which draws trainers and
facilitators from around the world. He set up the Institute after 30 years'
experience in international consulting and human resource management
positions in the UK, France, the United States and Switzerland – notably as
European Director of Executive Development with GTE in Geneva where he had training
responsibility for over 800 managers in 15 countries. John has published a number of
management and professional guides and regularly contributes articles to leading
management and training journals.

Many thanks to Richard Bradley of the Master Trainer Institute for helping these tips and
techniques come alive in the Management courses for participants from all over the world.
You can contact Richard at: Richard@mastertrainer.ch or www.mt-institute.com

ORDER FORM

Your details

Name _____

Position _____

Company _____

Address _____

_____

_____

Telephone _____

Fax _____

E-mail _____

VAT No. (EC companies) _____

Your Order Ref _____

Please send me:

	No. copies
The <u>Managing Difficult Participants</u> Pocketbook	☐
The _____ Pocketbook	☐
The _____ Pocketbook	☐
The _____ Pocketbook	☐

Order by Post
MANAGEMENT POCKETBOOKS LTD
LAUREL HOUSE, STATION APPROACH,
ALRESFORD, HAMPSHIRE SO24 9JH UK

Order by Phone, Fax or Internet
Telephone: +44 (0)1962 735573
Facsimile: +44 (0)1962 733637
E-mail: sales@pocketbook.co.uk
Web: www.pocketbook.co.uk

Customers in USA should contact:
Management Pocketbooks
2427 Bond Street, University Park, IL 60466
Telephone: 866 620 6944   Facsimile: 708 534 7803
E-mail: mp.orders@ware-pak.com
Web: www.managementpocketbooks.com

MANAGEMENT POCKETBOOKS